TERROR

Terror

TOBY MARTINEZ DE LAS RIVAS

FABER & FABER

First published in 2014
by Faber & Faber Ltd
Bloomsbury House
74–77 Great Russell Street
London WC1B 3DA

Typeset by Country Setting, Kingsdown, Kent CT14 8ES
Printed in England by Martins the Printers

A CIP record for this book
is available from the British Library

ISBN 978–0–571–29682–8

FSC
www.fsc.org
MIX
Paper from
responsible sources
FSC® C101712

2 4 6 8 10 9 7 5 3 1

Contents

Acknowledgements

Acknowledgements are due to the editors of the following publications where versions of these poems have appeared: *Ambit*, *The Best American Poetry*, *Black & Blue*, *Cimarron Review*, *Days of Roses*, *Eyewear*, *Night & Day*, *The OFI Press*, *Poetry* (*Chicago*), *Poetry London*, *Poetry Review*, *The Rialto*, *Selected Poems* and *The Wolf*.

'Three Illustrations from Blake's *Europe: A Prophecy*' was commissioned by the British Council on behalf of the Spanish Academy to celebrate the Spanish presidency of the EU in 2010.

I am grateful to the following organisations for their generous support: The Society of Authors for an Eric Gregory Award in 2005, Arts Council England for a Grants for the Arts award in 2010, and New Writing North for both the Andrew Waterhouse Award in 2008 and the Newcastle Australia Residency Award in 2013.

I would like to offer my deepest thanks to Professor Simon James, Dr Arin Keeble, Simona Noli, Oliver Hudson, G. C. Waldrep, Alfred Corn, Matthew Hollis, Martha Sprackland, David Harsent and Gillian Allnutt for their unstinting kindness, generosity and advice. And, finally, to Melanie Challenger for all of these, together with her invaluable correspondence since 2007.

Ignis

Twenty-One Prayers for Weak or Fabulous Things

As snow falls, as the first snow of this year falls & falls
    beyond all light & knowledge, I pray for Rufus
corrupted by lung parasites: whose viscera is corrupted
    & whose eyes are uncorrupted by flitting about
in the weak light. I speak this prayer into the black sun.

Secondly, I pray for David, who watches his dead sister
    wandering the yard each morning, up and down,
a shadow of herself. I pray for all things that slough off
    their skins: for snakes, for cicadas & silkworms
set doggedly to branches & pent in the rush of the bush.

Thirdly, I pray for a babbling, drunk fisherman wearing
    no trousers, dredged from the Tyne, who swore
ever after that by singing to Cuthbert he was able to call
    pearly trout from the river, to throw themselves
from their element into his – & there they flop, gasping.

Fourthly, I pray for a war protester, picketing The Sage,
    whose banners are scattered with cluster bombs
like falling seeds having the real viridian sting of black
    pansies closing. I pray for all things that unfurl
& shadow the sun: its star-track raked in the winter sky.

Fifthly, I pray for the ghost of Rene, & the living ghost
    of Mary in the final blank stage of Alzheimer's
nodding, clucking & fumbling. I pray for the sunflower,
    petals tight about a face of seed, head nodding
imperceptibly nightward. It has arms, too: to hold itself.

Sixthly, I pray for a pair of yellowhammers on the wire
    who sing in English: *a little bit of bread & no cheese.*
These are the hills. Not the north. This is upland chalks.
    I pray for the wild ghost of Barry MacSweeney
which has a bird's throat & thrumming, elliptical wings.

Seventhly, I pray for the sparrow with a slashed tongue,
    who in Egypt wore a jackal's garish blunt head
& ferried dead children across the river, but in England
    he's a happy, fat fellow. I listen to his declining
brotherhood at Broadway: there is one fewer every day.

Eighthly, I pray for Jimmy, who touches Mary's hands,
    & looks into Mary's empty shell each Thursday,
also on her birthday & the slow mornings of Christmas.
    The filament burns out its solitary candlepower.
8 is the sign for the infinite & is also the sum of YHVH.

Ninthly, I pray for the boy lying out in the summer rain
    by the old pigeon lofts round back of our house.
A boy: a father, but a boy too, failing to blink as globes
    of water drip into his eyes. To the moulting birds
he is a king at siege in the twinkle of his paraphernalia.

& I remember, one night when everyone was at the bar,
    opening up an eye in my wrist an inch & a half
back from the base of the thumb that glared left & right,
    then fixed itself faithfully on me, in my despite.
Kate, Kate. The morning gathered us in its white sheets,

white vestments, as when *Venus* in her burnished cleats
    drew out of Restronguet, the deep lines of linen
signalling cruelly from the shore as fog rose up like joy
    & a boisterous wind cuffed the heads off waves.
Tell this out, too: the curlew crying out over Culmhead.

Tenthly, I pray to the last few seconds of a cold August,
    when the world is silent, a sullen body of water
that brings the famished larva creeping to my fingertips,
    my tongue a water snail with soft horns forcing
its head from between my lips. Harp of dusk, & muscle.

My eleventh prayer is for Migdale checking the hooves
    of his sheep for rot peeling the hoof's heel, sole
& wall from their attachments to the foot: for the sheep
    like amputees lagging & nibbling at lung flukes
& brain worms: & some fall down in the clart, shaking.

My twelfth prayer is for the unfledged rooks overcome
    by ants beneath the high nests. For the membra
over the pods of their eyes. For the shine of their beaks
    & the orbit. For the boot I bring down on them.
Let me love best all these creeping things that creepeth.

My thirteenth prayer is to the ghost of Nicholas of Flüe,
    who saw the face of the Lord lacerated with fury,
& whose own face was fixed into a mask by that vision.
    The faint shapes of his children, flinching away.
Today even the little sparrow cannot bear to look at me.

My fourteenth prayer is for you, Isa, altered by distance.
    I see your heart, & it has the shape of the winter
cherry convulsing in the gale. Arterial web of branches,
    blossom battered off, acquiescence in the bough.
But mine is a bird fixed in the canopy – a false lapwing.

Sometimes, when we touch, you subtly shift your body
    ten degrees to the right or left – so it is your hip
or thigh, & not your genitals which shiver against mine:
    we do not stand dovetailed, as the beating wing
should to the physicality of lift. Or the wall to its brace.

My fifteenth prayer is for the recoiling bee that I found
    in the allotment, like a small aeronaut slumped
in the burst spars of his machine. He thumped his sting
    once into the sodden ground to vent his temper
& is free to go. A cold season gathers itself in the earth.

And did I tell you about Burgess the miner, who tossed
          the body of his daughter into the gut of the well
at Watercombe & married her stepmother in the woods:
          he was caught out by the deadlight that winked
above the shaft: & a sheep rustler spied her down there.

Here they call a deadlight a spunky, the ghost of a child
          that catches & flares above a tract of still water.
On Midsummer they gather at church to meet the souls
          of the freshly buried, & invite each one to swell
their companies: but some of these I blame on the cider.

My sixteenth prayer is for the drunk staggering through
          a shattered gate in Thomas Bewick's tail-piece:
after the merganser ascetically rearranging its plumage,
          after the mute swan riding from its harbourage
like a troubled schooner. & in the sky – a double moon.

My seventeenth prayer is to the memory of Christopher
          Smart kneeling in a torrent of bees at Staindrop
to pray, or cutting the Song to David into the bare page
          of a wall with a claspknife & a splinter of glass,
& with his fingertip rubbing charcoal into the scratches.

My eighteenth prayer is for the glass ghosts of Leopold
          & Rudolf Blaschka, combinations of moonlight
& organ, slight tendrils of glass teasing out their quarry
          by tentacle & night vision. The Scyphomedusa
flows above us, a star in a doomed pod or constellation.

My nineteenth prayer is for the one who kept his watch
          on the stair the night we brought the bairn back,
the iron of whose glare counteracts supernatural malice.
          After the owl & dragon, he is the most puissant
& canny of all living beasts. The devil cannot pass him.

My twentieth prayer is for the wind sobbing in the haw,
     & the lamb that lurches through the Pentateuch.
Tobe, Tobe, you have called him here to face the music
     & be thrust face down in the beck, shorn of life,
the tongues of water whispering its lineage into his hair.

Last, I pray for the makers of prayers, which are poems
     we say to ourselves in the hard times, dry times,
cold times. In tenements, in tower blocks, in the locked
     tin caskets of our hearts. In the darkness, falling
& falling like snowflakes beyond all light & knowledge.

Simonsburn

When this comes

The yews like sentinels, divested of life, bristling with dull pods or cherries
of blood,

                    at the lych gate, in the city of the dead.

One day, I shall have a daughter I will call out *Honey* to,

                           or *Oh, Hon,*

phonemes beyond approximation in the strict textures of print, half exaltant
or dramatic address, half strangulation.

Oh, the feminised rhetoric of pleading, knees cleft in the unlight
at Simonsburn, the poisonous frill of nettles purring in the wind.

Dire and beautiful is the male voice in its unmanning: Alessandro Moreschi,
Hostias et Preces, from far away and through static.

Stripped of its sexual function, something cries through the open mouth *Óh,*

Óh, Óh, unrepeatably, consubstantial with desire. Believe me,

           in the carnal paradise, you still can dance with terrific abandon.

When that comes

Penitential Psalm

Tenderly

Out of the shallows, horizonless, unbroken, the impenitent, vertical body
tenders its asperities

to blinding waters.

None to anoint it, looking out towards Huish and the dismal stratocumuli.

O, hark at! The helicopterish *whap | whap* of goose wings.

Shall I thrust

my own head under, inhale the shattered meniscus,

ghost-cases of larvae fixed to stems in the vacancy of self-possession
the third clause held indefinitely to spite your transformational grammar?

Fierce joy that is like retching, undo me. As a dead polity,

brick by brick, stitch by stitch, the squat, feudal tower at Langport,
or the drowned mole in this baptismal water, claws subtly demonstrative

of admonishment, supplication, *woefully arrayed*.

My tender heartroot for thee brake:
My tender heartroot for you in the brake of thorns,
and the desperate purchase of this falling metre, Laura.

[9]

Three Illustrations from Blake's *Europe: A Prophecy*

Frontispiece

Kneeling in *contrapposto*, the shoulders and arms
Twist against the swelling vertical axis of the left leg.
Muscles set in shadow and raucous, oppositional light.
This is one aspect of the ideal nude: arrayed as man,
Pre-democratic and wholly local, wholly sufficient.
The borrowed contortions, the splayed web of fingers
Or wind-blasted hair raddled with age, feebly white.
Heaven adorned with fire, darkness divided against
Itself where he leans to set the bright stars and the law.
Delicate sash of eyelids half closed in concentration.
And what this posture connives with is what is in us,
Is what we are: inexorable, self-willed bowing down.

Plate VIII

Hold yourself to yourself, my lost and keening one.
Beyond this room, and this fire, and this infant body
Stretched in abject stillness on the floor, lies nothing
But the failed State, arming itself against consolation.
What does she want, this duchess, in the blue lustre
Of her robes, if not to tax you to death and eat you,
A ring of white pearls at her beating, heron's throat
As the cruel and oblatory smoke ascends in clouds?
Who can doubt, now, that he foresaw and foreheard
The full range of tragedy: Passchendaele and Omaha,
Torrejón de Ardoz, Guernica: that in my grandfather's
Throat seemed the vocables of a paradisal language?

Plate XVII

Jerusalén. Of which the stylobate at extreme left
Is surely an outrider, the suburbs of the Holy City.
Look at the purpose in the eye of this tall, naked boy,
His right leg planted on the bottom step, his lover
Upon his shoulders, his massive torso twisted to drag,
From the following flames, his bairn, his daughter.
This is the ideal nude: not arrayed in flesh, but really
Flesh: sprung from earth, newly risen, individuated.
Beneath whose bare foot the secularity of stone rests
Its cold and dependable mass, begging to be shaped.
He shall make of his own arms a fold, that the gale
May pass them by, the fire not bite them with its teeth.

Covenant

Say the truth. Northumberland as Israel. Parts of it prefigured as the Shulamite woman. Hebron, hard by Haltwhistle.

Robert Westall, at the texts of *The Plague House* and *Machine Gunners.*
The grey hull of *Resurre.*

Or *The Wind Eye*, in these fallen days.

Reading this text to my sons, as if wading through harl into his strange, apostolic light.

O, Shulamite.

It is a wild fucking kingdom.

Surface bewildered by the risen heads of seals, a sea trout's dorsal arc. The thistle, garishly dressed, rehearses its gospel crowned in flame.

World, split between shod and unshod.

The King of Scotland, dead.

Terror and counter-terror, broken walls littering the dominion,
the high woe of bairns like seal-pups.

Marram grass soup,
no less.

I must bend my knee to him again.

Clouds shift like tercels inland, upland, west to Gateshead, and the rain in its vehemence.

Crede

Judas as a secret Messiah forgoing the garden of the nihilists for a branch of the tree.

The body as miniaturised image of the state, inviolate.

Tyler's vision of the commons, burned before the king at Smithfield, to his satisfaction.

On the road to Northumberland, John Ball's *envois*, little admonishments in code.

I have pled I might not always be a shaking reed.

I believe in a hell most nearly seen in Doré's sixty-seventh illustration of *The Inferno*.

Three isolated words: *Kornblumenblau, Sparhauke* and *Availeth*.

Philip Hughes on Everlasting Death, I take so much
to heart.

The bleat, desperate.

stoven
Tumbled stells, the razed sheepfold that is our northern image of the body of Christ.

One bitter season before two
sweet.

Fluorspar, correlative to purging fire.

swaying purple
Furthermore, bright fields of rape, the trampled nests among the thistleheads, alleluia.

The Clean Versus the Psoriatic Body

The body as image of the state, violated and violating.

in the hindquarters

Broken & brought to heel in its northernmost parts, and the dykes like scars, *wasta est*.

The moon above Alston, which is an anagram of the end, where my heart was lost.

That hé said: *I do will it*, and meant it.

Your head, de Comines.

The exultant, levelling teeth of the harrow biting at the meat of this pale heaven.

Torn open, suzerain.

My little sons are lain out side by side in winter, the light barely born, that it might not burn.

And my bride has lain with another.

Not bough snow, nor flawless mirror of the fall, nor allergic to September.

Not an iconoclast, not an islander, not England in miniature.

Nor does he hear how the sea hisses, that shall salt and scorn and whiten me.

From the runnels in spate at Alston, petal, to the bare, shaking Levels.

where my heart was lost

My citadels, and my drowned folds. My fields,

my arms, my brutalist heartland, the corporations of London that humbled Napoleon.

Poem, Three Weeks After Conception

The sky will be shaped like a bow when you crane your neck to pray into it.
Roofless, but not burned. Though black, spangled.

Your hair will be the white spray at High Force,
teeth pebbles in the vent.

You will escape the ogre of psoriasis that lives on the knees,
elbowcaps, genitals and face.

For you the stars have already locked into place.

For you the blue coltsfoot in the allotment will be an electrical wonder.

The Red Kite, wolf and bear will return to the borders in numbers.

You will be buried in a country far away, a country like home,
of absolute rainfall.

Beneath a late moon, unfurling.

You shall witness the domination of Jerusalem.

The capsize of London.

I pray that I will never hit or humiliate you,
for whom the best wine in the world will be pressed in Kent.

Who will live to see supermarkets dictating military policy to governments.

Our Lady of Gateshead, watch over us.

Things I Have Loved

The Flea, principally,
pronounced *Flay*.

Smart, who disliked clean linen,
whom Johnson would as lief pray with as anyone.

Paper aeroplanes like prayers in childhood, winged, rising, risen.

Headflare in multi-directional light, that Blackdown morning
the lamb was born, dead, beside his sister.

XXVI March,
the jute-sack and the shovel, as if by magic.

My never-to-be-born daughter, of the House of Míro Quesada.

How her body bucked like a beast dragged by its neck from the holt
when I touched it as instructed.

Each breath, a mist or brief rapt element, swept up,
escaped.

Fenlight, shivering in its seat.

Blackdown Song

In front of the gate whose tubes hummed in the wind
like owls hooing each other across a dark field, Isabel,
was the firepit's tract of soot-soft & snow-white ashes.

It went deeper than you knew, after years of bonfires,
dusks when sightly wings of paper flared in a woosh
of sparks & ghosted into darkness like minor stars.

Beyond the singing gate lay the dark field which ate
the bodies of lambs & threw up the bleached fans
of pigeon wings: the grass grew red in those places.

I dug the pit with a shovel & scooped bucketloads
to feed my father's garden which drew down silver
mouthfuls of ash & the tangled brown potato haulms.

All the while the gate hummed tunelessly in the wind:
tunelessly, but with range: high & low, long & short,
disconnected, artless, dumb life struggling into song.

I struck so reckless, Isabel – hot, one-handed, peeved,
& clanged a rock that hung in earth as consciousness
is said to inhere in the self, the self to hang in the body.

High, low, long, short. My arms went dead, a dazed bird
burst from my skull – the rock humped, deaf to the blow.
A brilliant ringing in the blade secured itself to that axis.

Shiggaion

the bare naked field is thy part, as
    the cat all eyes and bemes and flame
couches into the shell of that vexed
    gorgeous chest, she is a rose, is a for-

knowing beyond *thee*, colossal in
    thy ignorance, *thy* field blight, as *thy*
black stinking potatoes, *thy* silt,
    alii dicebant haec verba non sunt dae-

monium habentis numquid daemo-
    nium potest caecorum oculus aperire.
Wildfire sheering the high margins
    of the road where nothing in chains,

another day rising, a man teetering
    on the edge of a desk on tiptoes, feet
scrabbling, his neck is in a noose,
    such is *thy* part, crownede wyth reytes,

bere mee to thy leathall tyde, bear
    me, if you can and if the back straight
as a buttercup stalk permits you, if
    it is allowed & approved by communal

delete all reference to such, sinful,
    man is alone, so scuttle back & forth
across my patriotic Brunel Clifton
    bridge of a riveted back, the rest sold,

here is the sink of my, my stinking
    vulgate body, *dicebant autem multi ex*
ipsis daemonium habet et insanit
    quid eum auditus, it is the dogma, it is

the capital has done this to my so
   shining brow, Blodewydd, rendering
the glue from the butchered bone
   boiling down the surplus immaterial

capital of a nation: you want, you
   buy it, why should I say one direct
thing, why? Does the goshawk, its
   wingtip pivoting around the inward

arc of its turning circle as the finch
   breaks cover from beneath the tarred
bird table, authentic rural design,
   the serried fir trees as dead in the land

as their tenders care a shite for the
   for the proper grammar? It *is* grammar,
the purity of design, the framework
   shaking, never collapsing until finally

permitted to do so. So you stitch
   your hair, my graceful fled love, and so
everything is the winterlong flight
   of certain flowers and birds I can't name

and am proud to do so. The bridge
   is depravity, the road, the government,
the centre of fear and betrayal, just
   act within your proscribed bounds, as

the goshawk and the leaping joyful
   cat refuse to do, beak & teeth in the crop
and the bright blood, foamy as alco-
   hol, the darling berries in October again –

that is how it all was and will never
    never be, *facta sunt autem encenia in Hiero
solymis et hiemps erat.* The going
    down of that eyelid, and it was winter.

Natura

To narrate is to relent: in me there shall be no relenting,
storm baiting the fields with light, the deathless instant
of outhouses, cars prone on gravel in searing greyscale,
the copse hard by the storage tank deepening its covert.
Who steps with me into the shadows, allegiant, sudden, if not
you, from the foothills out across the bare Levels,
the briefest image regnant even at the point of collapse.
Now turquoise lightning thrusts among the stark ridges,
the water discloses in a moment the shape of its tresses,
the torn birch is lashed, stumbles, immaculate with fire.   *Station III*
                                                    desolate

Père

Nothing before or since so clear as this: the windshield
iridescent, the heads of sainfoin in blazing brightwork,
a little Duke of Burgundy recumbent on whitlow-grass
sumptuous in its slashed doublet of dun-and-tangerine.
I might be betraying him the simplicity of his pleasure,
this man I rarely knew unguarded, his binoculars tilted
to the silhouettes of Phantoms like flies on the horizon.
Far-sighted, in the manner of Père Chérubin d'Orléans.
Half-leant against the searing bonnet in a frazzled shirt,
in old blue boxer-shorts with the cock-hole stitched up.

Boscombe

Armour is noon that may withstande his wounde

Noonlight deadened on armour, turbofans reverberant:
what glory is still in the world holds fast to that image.
How the decorous aurora or neuron-cloud or whatever
it is haloing the cow parsley shudders in the crosswind,
high cirrus burned away yet re-gathering continuously
at the notion of his grace, self-generative, unobliterate,
of doubtful substance in our narrowing fields of vision.
Hosanna the does frozen forty yards shy of the runway,
the scream of turbofans decelerating as if the last days
had come upon us and the trumpets rang *tarari*, *tarara*.

Futility of representation, of image, cherubic shepherd.
Only the irradiate Inmaculada of Nagasaki can help us,
or Bonhoeffer on the forsaken God, on hís decrepitude.
Le Pont des Tourelles, buckling under the concussions.
Orléans, in conflagration. And this, a four-square stable
in the hinterland of assault, thick stands of corn waded
through by cows in labour, the one who told this to me
easing his eye cautiously to the door to find two horses
in yoke at the *charette*, each knelt on its cannon-bones
as if sleeping, unscathed, groomed, dead in their traces.

Untitled

Poetic space here signifies *page* in London, a language
I only half speak. Ah, Blanchot, these heaving galleries,
rats in tortoiseshell nerd-glasses, reproduction Jacobite war-
apparel and spadrilles, pathetically self-indentured.
Re-imagine all the bitter works of redemption as cheap
aesthetic, historical suffering assuaged as literary trope,
Purcell's death chants piped over the duct-taped rubble,
and you glimpse hell as it really is: not swathed in fires,
but overflowing with diversion, its connate bankruptcy
& anguish – or whatever it denotes, this tenacity of loss.

Ptuj

Párasites. But yóu, wiped, polychromatically hungover,
the exposed décolletage manifesting slight sun damage
falling and lifting, cowled swan-head of the pubic bone,
eyes, that òpen, were of such a violent and comely blue,
my own reft self in the spectral disk of each iris, clósed.
Christ, through these daytimes I have bleated after you,
missed you, fetched a species of hell down on my folks.
Lá, d'you remember how the rain stumbled down on us,
and we dumped the others and scuttled home through it.
Oh Tobe, why can't you shut yr goddamn hole for once.

Coldsong

The clear eye that ponderously, faithlessly refuels itself,
sexually acquisitive, incalescent at the sites of betrayal.
What power art thou that from below has made me rise . . .
Guess you need to hear it in Nomi's cold counter-tenor.
Or Thomas Sackville on sleep, the three most beautiful
verses in English. Side by side with this Lá, there steps
something approaching agony, comically misrehearsed.
Heedless ides of our days. And down the rain did drum.
Lá, hís love is not our love, in constancy and affection,
but as the wind that thrashes the maple, then withdraws.

Recessionary

Dual carriageway plashed with reds: the pearlescence
of the kestrel peering through each foaming wingbeat,
cars slashing through run-off inertial at the downshift.
In heofonlic leoht, the citadel crouches behind smoke,
dwindling, the unbowed, brittle lime sheathed in frost.
See all these things as they might appear in retrospect:
self-possessed, harkened to, clad in negative radiance,
the snow prolific but not annihilating, the tear-jerking
wind, the clarts: or see this as a measure of restitution,
where the harrow in tarps discreetly bares its anorexia.

take me up

Ἔσχατου

If this is midsummer, then our three hours of darkness
have begun. London, you go down kiteless in yr steels
and pre-eminence, those funny little parks eradicating
power walkers in swathes of false blossom, those post-
industrial duplexes bowed towards their supermarkets.
I do not spare myself from this, stooping carnifex, nor
the city rats in their suits of fur paddling through urine,
their resurrected hours peerless until called to account.
In the dictatorship of illusion, nightfall is halogenated,
barren. There is a hill far away: Gateshead the Golden.

cast me aside

Annulment

What might or may the sely larke say

I feared the water: the shadows and spawn resurrecting
in dark light, the glory-stare through low broken cloud.
Genuflecting among the basal leaves of withering hare-
bells, I saw and see the barred and agile God ravenous
in hís snowdrift of feathers tearing at the plucked anus,
prolific eye engulfing the days, the years turned briefly
to a psalmody of rotor blades behind the sheltering hill.
And something else: the prodigious bellowing of cows
in the yard planting their bulks and straining after their
penned weans: that still reaches me from a way aways.

Look, it is March as it always is, the disordered spectra
rainbowed in wet asphalt or else invisible, hi-vis power
walkers buried in music jerking their heads defensively
in time, pitbulls barely tethered, the clotted buds of ash
groping to-usward, salvation's blind or suffering intent.
Also in time: the supernumerary rainbows stanchioned
in glassy shallows overflying both Huish and Langport
reassert their covenant: are, were, overbearingly bright
signals of conviction, promissory against black nimbus.
As Neruda's *violeta*, self-collapsing. In *corolla of rage.*

Psoriatic bough snow, dessicate blossom reconfigured
in a vortex, transluminous grass-heads blighted with it,
the muzzled Alsatian whining through her death mask
at wasps: in bitterness the almonds are rigging the hills.
That I have kept a tiny and concealed speck of myself
innocent through sexual betrayal, through punishment,
that I am in my marrow a physical coward, I find hard
to reconcile with any notion of mercy or assuagement
justly made: nor do I see what authority this disclosure
holds in nature, beyond a plaintive and facile catharsis.

Gehenna

My uttermost music will be whining or agonal gasping,
unadorned plainchant of approximants, barely stressed.
Do not tell this, but I come awake at times, the burning
rick in my head, the flayed tarpaulin risen in vehement
admixtures of wheat and plastic, plus several panicked
cut-outs lumbering through mown stalks backlit by fire
cursing down phones, or holding still with lit cigarettes
in formal postures of despair: bereft, as those that slept
the hour, hair luminously thinned, shabbily bejacketed.
In the dying marches of hís night, keep your watch late.

Lá, in the dead marches

Woolbury

Óh, Óh, Óh, the fritillary sunning itself on nightshade,
photovoltaic fan of the wing-array twitched open shut
open in spasmodic adoration, chalk radiant in furrows,
the world aglow, preparatory, not yet in conflagration.
Unbroken pa, my balsawood chuck glider is crowning
the thornbush, ungetdownable, the sun amassing itself
in the leading edge, wedged by the wind, driven upon.
God, how the brain beats stripes out of itself, the body
unsalveable, stunned in its tree. I am heartily sorry for
my fault, my offence. All that is in me spells its dread.

Hurry

And Purgatory not as excarnation, not as final theosis,
but here and inwardly among the penultimate realities,
the stillness that presages παρουσία, the widening eye
of the storm that shall churn lime leaves to fish-scales,
narratives and counter-narratives in abrupt contention,
weathervanes spun wailing through their many points.
Oh pa, behold yr son in the dazzling mirror of his self-
regard, flung through that glass, unanchored, as chaff.
I had a suit to plead: but so much of the summer wind
tilts in my mouth, I cannot set one word down straight.

Chasse

In that sense, I am less a facsimile than a simulacrum of myself unfallen, made in that image, razored Book of Hours face-up in fragments of windowglass, *scène de chasse* as primary illustration, the pulsing emerald of the oak, squealing boarlets, dogs snapping at a doe half sunk in flowers, huntsmen *en fête* lifting clarions to the stilled havoc of air: say January, the sun falling beneath a superimposed zodiac, larks snagged in nets weeping, venting that famous tongue: the tongue that is so gently spoken at times, so pathetically adequate.

Renovatur

The English Garden as Political Art

The cock pheasant, spectral in white rain. Deft admonitory hole of the eye. Unsheathed from its costly scabbard, the downswept white bone of the spur, terrible in its way

From the first, I wanted to be a gunsmith: temperer, bluer of steel. The pale light in my armoury plain-to-a-fault, Protestant light, sufficient to itself, as it is in the tongue of Anne Bradstreet

Stuntless growth of early May, where, in the ideal, the lamb might lie beside the vixen, at the nipple of the vixen, or a martin dip her beak between the teeth of hungry rats

But winter is the loosener of snares, & the deadfall of my strength

Very Rich Hours

Winter. The forest. Deerhounds at butchery. Heaven's gold leaf flywheel plunging over the tower: *La demeure de plusiers seigneurs, chevaliers et autres ses mieux aimées*

Those several lords & their friends: how they flushed the quarry from its covert, too, on the last frozen morning of the failed century & burst the pack like a bow-wave through the ditches

Upturned faces, cogent & frighteningly blank. They were listening for their Lord, the cry & tread of the master, his reckless overstriding the fences, his will at the bitter end

The heart, the hemmed fox, sustained & broken by its flight

The Superabundance of the Real Presence

Though the verb *to be*, like all copulas, is static as a penned bull, I haul a frail bulk to its knees, first, then feet, & thunder through the street. I am the unpenned bull of the Lord

Whose name confounds me. That is the hunger of women. That is mercy & condemnation. That bore the quail & the shotgun. That is the leaf of the tongue flickering in her mouth's gospel

Perpetuum mobile. The days. The riddle canons & Fludd's waterscrew. The sinking into: all his. Likewise rats, the self hanging from a tree, de Chardin's *immortal centre of love*

That bore the sparrowhawk that harbours winter in the covert of its wing

ix xi

Skull of a Rat, Museum of Antiquities, Newcastle-upon-Tyne

That suffered the wind, the rain, a hod of corn vulgar with ergot. Knew what it meant to break cover & scuttle
beneath the gale of talons, the tailfeathers' ineluctable airbreak

In the stubble-burning days, I hunted rats with a break-barrel .177, hunched in the dark, for what gleam would
break from the eye, & when it did, I, black cloud, swallowed that moon

Stand now in the field of its disregard, eyes portals to a place where nothing is fledged nor can find its fastness,
no north, no south, no east, no west. Bone pall, unshattered yet

Brittle scoured cauldron of his spite

Water

In the blue plastic water butt, a false night quivers with larvae: fear wakens in a face that ignores me for the sky, unsmiling, ringed by a halo the bud-headed branches creep into

Something clarified in her in the last days, recalling her brother's consumption, her own face barely held above dark & rising water: how it had been a kind of public drowning by proxy

In the night a family of foxes gathers to drink in the ditch, the water struck by stars & streaked with filth, & one freezes & glares across the divide like the widow's boy at Nain

Pray for us now, & at the hour of our life

Pyropsalm

Separate. Radically alone, even inside each other. Physical bliss equals extinction. Reach your hand into the fire.
Among these ruins the analogue of flesh kneels for grace

Listen. The blackbird that screams at the terror of the morning. The disorder of its syntax. Poor bairn. It screams
to hear itself. This is the affliction pride, or its corollary, self-chastisement

The tongue's ferocity & exactions. English as the first language of nature. Its denotion of self: vertical, lowering,
isolate. Unblent, unbearable in the tower of its resolution

How far have I fallen? My fontanelle is still open

Through the Window into the Garden that was His Last Sight

Buds for the XVII March, which is also my son's birthday. Roseate, lipped nipple-heads. Irresolute pane of sky, iron-grey, forthcoming of rain, but brushed by early sun

Rotor blades slapping the air in hurt spin their little fishcan eastward with doleful coughs. Do not turn from this, nor the wire, nor the mole-traps that disgorge their gorgeous treasures

Do not turn from them though they waver & diminish in the fundamental blank of the eye, beacons of vacillate, scared light, or the unrehearsable memory of being born

The gravel beds beyond them, & beyond them, the cress beds

Birth Riddle

I write this on the XVII March, which is the day I brought you into the world to die. Indeed, I thought you were dead. I shall become, now, as the tamed & hooded Lanner

In the vision of the German Master, Christ is carved from a single blank of oak caparisoned in blood, swooning. You were that blank, bar the pan-shaped fracture depressing the paddle of the foot

All that persists of heaven flows across the closed square of the absolute window. Acute, cold, utterly relentless lance in the stanchless flank, pre-ordained & unforseeable

XVII unjumbled is VIXI. The crosstrees of the blank hold. The thief must turn his head

The Male Understanding of Devotion

I write this in the ninth year of the endless war. On the XXVII February & third consecutive day without sun. This is what sinks in me: a millstone done with grinding

Words that flutter without thought. The Saker, the Lanner & the Barbary. Grouped absent-mindedly in threes with obsolete, feminine endings. There is no assuagement left in them

In me there is assuagement. From nightfall's angel, the hawk within the clouds that does not miss, but stoops & makes off with the children of whomsoever it pleases

But I shall be as a shield to you & keep the shadow from off your back

The Primacy of Physical Pain

Now the Lightning, the angel, must suffer us at its nudity & ascent. Gaunt, light-bearing rage. Gravity's denials.
The fenced observation bay, Boscombe. Eighty six or seven

English Electric. Sold, finally, to the Procurator Venal. Who here of my generation remembers the silver shock
cone & vertically stacked engines? The pikeish ventral tank, pillars of flame

O, Da, Dad, Daddy. What do I call you now? You remember. Larks in panic worrying the grassheads, the trilled
alarms as its roar of pain thinned to a high, bestial whistling

Thus shall our shapes rise & dwindle from the eye

The Fish-hook

Not perpetual. Marked. I fail the words or they fail me, but: I am not *failed by*. Bestowal under duress undoes most of us & the bullfrog guffaws in triumph from the path

This is where hé died: in the garden, at the point of election. Stiffened, as if barbed metal. Now I see the body as that: cold, lost: but not beyond recall, for hís promise is the failsafe, surely

Love, the silence grows visible between us, its starvation calls to you like the quail that from its clutch of eggs rises & peeps to draw the quick scarlet fox off into darkness

Not *failed by*. Not that passivity, surely

Allegory of Faith with Hunting Goshawk

Carmona's *Allegory of Faith*, a frozen, bodiless woman half suffocated by the veil that might be a shroud, must be a shroud, for her eyes of stone, it is clear, see nothing

I, too, wear the veil of stone. In my carriage of maleness, I am his radiant bride, bisexual as death. In the liftings I saw the weird, fluted breast array of a Goshawk striking in Blackdown light

& a Lanner once, at a distance, I can't be sure. Beyond that, nothing. It is ignorance, finally, I settle heavily into, blind, unearned wanting for his bodiless touch, restitution

This is a poem, if by that you mean a hopeful & hopeless reckoning

After Reading Philip Hughes on Everlasting Death

Nothing is let go. Not the Gyrfalcon, not the sinner. Though its logic holds faster than eternal pain, in which law might eternal destruction figure as condign punishment?

In newly wreckable light, shotguns sob across the Levels, lead shot cascading in the broken well of the morning, wild pigeons folding their wings forever on the upstroke & falling away

Is this the shifting syntax of reasonable self-doubt or a failure to hold fast? As firstly, I cannot shut my ears to it, & secondly, I cannot look it in its rapidly focussing eye

Hoy this in the gutter. Nothing is let go

On the day chi-ch'ou, the Sun was eclipsed, and it became dark in the daytime. The Empress Dowager was upset by it and her heart was ill at ease. Turning to those around her she said, 'This is on my account.'

SZU-MA CH'IEN, *Shih-chi*
in F. RICHARD STEPHENSON, *Historical Eclipses and Earth's Rotation*

Who is this who is coming

ISAIAH 63:1

Integra

Lines of Geese

(*clouds*)

And gebide þe þoune priwa east and cwaeð priwa:
There should be viciousness in seeing – a deep cold light that takes no account
of suffering or hope: that is neither itself
nor our relation to it,
now I number the names of my own children among the incarnations of ruin.
A panic of feathers whitens my mind as with snow,
I still can never forget Wesley on the proper station of the worm
among the genera of the final restitution,   *the yolk of the pasqueflower that failing, blazes upon*
                                                      both lamb and tiger
nor
the evergreen that stands self-
assured in its hauberk
of wind

(*clouds*)

Christina Rossetti

Say this: there ís, there ís recompense for bodily suffering, or there is no justice.
Between Monna Innominata (*Come back to me,*
who wait and watch for you –)
& Monna Innominata (*'I, if I perish, perish'* –
Esther spake:),
the, óh the, óh the | bríght snóws evaporate as though they had never been,
a subtle frost withdraws –
the tree that might stand for sexual yearning or the body
re-substantialised after judgement
belongs
abundantly to its last things: unruined, vestal,
touched by the shepherd she was blind to
& vividly foresaw

(clouds)

(clouds)

blind shepherd of our darkness

Or say thís: ἀγάπηη is subordinate to justice, the moment of redemption not felt as love,
but a self-righting by which hé might,
without guilt, look us
in the eye.
I concede the possibility that,
stating this,
I thrust my self head-first into perdition's featureless, intense
claustrophobia.
Across
the snowfield, muted calls:
the vitreous idiolect of an accipiter
veiled in snow
conjures its obsolete paradise
from
the wastes.
Don't tell me what I mean, or,
in malice, comfort
me.
Òur dárkness –
bone
what else can I say from the jewelled hibernacle of my doubt.
In truth, the snow accumulates
& drifts at will,
a 'difference-in-the-world' – a difference,
surely –
the yew absénted, yard ŏblítèrăte.
Come to see that, now – only terror that is all-abiding, & this formal counterpoint to it.

(clouds)

Easter Sunday, Plaza de la Magdalena, Córdoba

(clouds)

Girls in communion dresses white as death, the boys in spotless faux militaria
step from the porch hand
in hand
stunned, for a second, in the sudden access
of light.
A cold wind needles the pine,
the crocus
in her hood of pinks
shivers.
Between the black traceries of the bench, a clutch
of broken eggs spill
their albumen:
beneath,
a nest despoiled by cats,
the half-trimmed
box
hedge they glare from forlorn, and slightly absurd.
This is all, at its heart, still
Primo de Rivera's:
still discreetly
whistling
me hallará la muerte si me lleva,
still listening out
for Tallería's massed trumpets *con brio*
with interjections of swirling
flute, –
do you know *Soleá* | it is
beautiful,
the lemon tree, and the white well. Night waits all day in the boughs of the fir.

(clouds)

Easter Sunday, Plaza de San Lorenzo, Córdoba

(*clouds*)

I have been so tired,

Lá The tremulous canticle of an ambulance as it gravitates between cowering cars,
    chassis bowing left | then right on parabolic
    leaf springs.
    Sumptuous as Negroli's burgonet,
    crepis sancta
    damascenes the stubborn sheets of failing masonry,
    the armoured veil of each involucrum
    grips a pale head
    and lowers
    it,   *Selah*   *i*
    swifts in their black velocities
    dart like fish among
    seedlets.   *Selah*
    The moue of a swallow in passing, basal phalanxes
    skimming her cradle
    the earth,   *Selah*   *ii*
    this unharvested plague of oranges
    that stand
    for our love season after season too bitter for words
    or use.   *Selah*
             bocca chiusa
    I say this: hís *Offenbarsein*
    is manifest less
    in hís rising and our knowledge of it   *iii*
    than in the eye's fatal
    cold calculus.
    What is truer, or more total than my final blindness?
    Ελπίδα: Ελπίδα
    ïs trùer,
    neither apparent | nor concealed. Gód, I have loved so mány things in the dust.

(*clouds*)

Easter Sunday, Plaza de San Rafael, Córdoba

(clouds)

Listen,

The song-finch flaunts a gorgeous alarum – though he is not much to look at,
pompous little *señor* with his breeches
and sententious
gut.
Disparaging of the bougainvillea, the hoarse children – yet
something distinctly female
clings to him:
as if his voice were split, and the other –
strange, bisexual Gretchen
at her treadle –
cried
Sein Händedruck, und ach,
sein Kuß!
Old men are charmed, gripping their canes and white teeth.
Distantly, the city is
ringing.
Doves in bibs sodden with motor diesel sail from minarets,
the faces of roses inscrutable
as martyrs.
muta Do
not think there is no pain in hím,
that hé is not wretched
with
yearning –
in Jeremiah the image of Ephraim steps, breaking hís heart.
From the cloacae
of doorways
dance
white blossoms that gather the wind | the morning ríses from its cóma of bélls.
turbulent   *Lá*

(clouds)

Triptych for the Disused Non-Conformist Chapel, Wildhern

Patricia Beer

From the deep harbour ἀρτταγησόμεθα: we shall be caught up.   *O Lord thou draggest me out*
Plymouth as it was, the Hoe laid out above Goemagot
chary with scattered primrose, a stand of tulips
that court the sun as glacially as girls beneath rayon doll-hats
and parasols inclining to passersby on the promenade.
Beyond the breakwater, *Warspite* between *Grenville* and *Hood*.
Narrow-eyed gulls with heartrending mews like paramours.
Then Padua, balanced upon its own rubble. Raw colours
returning with the first days of spring unkempt and ravenous
to the faculty, students linking arms with practised ease
in giro through a stream of bicycles trilling in sweet voices.
Kisses desired in full view returned, the elegant cafés
audible from the river where the sky wanders through its city.
Austen and Gaskell. Coffee, a stroll. Austen again. Brontë.

I met her. The grey, lavish eyes. A ruthless stare softened
by an accent. She was gracious, even to my callow posturing –
called one windy effort that ended *O Lord thou draggest me out*
a *most faithful homage to Eliot*, grave with kindly mockery.
I drank my bitter tea. But consider this: her calves in sheer silk
still a girl's, her polished tan half-heels set against them:
magnificent. That Italian air, the strict bob ordering her face.
And driving back with Pinkie at his schoolmasterly pace,
I picked my nails and watched myself in the dark wing when
The King in Thule suddenly swelled with falling cadence
through the speakers, its pure aurality heralding
the shattering white late snow of April, the road a vein
of black ore exhausting itself slowly to the north,
the fields at Rogationtide empty, innocent of all things, even life.

      i   *ii*   *iii*

Fay Pomerance

Beneath the shadow of his wings, the scales stand baited against us.
Maddox, charming predator, robustly mustachioed, vivid
behind thick lenses condemning that *discredited iconography* –
towers collapsing through quicksand, pavanes of anguish,
the bodies of the lost ransacked by hobgoblins –
reclines, his hatred virtue, its vital purity and strength,
all his outrage told against those *humiliating genuflections.*
Since there is no model for her features, conceive of her
blanched as the Cabbage White, each brush-stroke the drama
of a tiny kenosis, the bright clatter of ferrules over-
heard as conversation at a distant table, queasy and isolating –
Babel. Tower of teacups at ominous angles in the studio,
rings indelibly stamped in the watercolour paper's grain.
Stretched in membranes of fat: passover, Lamb. Burning leaven.

Head ringing with psilocybin and gin, I kneel in the foreground
of my own life quarter-sized, self-consciously humbled,
like the donor in Altdorfer's *Crucifixion* peering through
the shadow of the cross to the city emptied of daylabourers
that rides at ease in the sun, bay deliciously windswept,
the curdled blue of high summer fading
out beyond the spruce where she stands in her living robes –
and still I cannot comprehend how incidental we are
to our own redemption, though the sacrifice remains intimate
in violence, the half-accepting flinch of the face
as if breasting the parapet or tensed into the impact
of a tube train, the rapt mother in the privacy of her distress.
Here is the gate of horn, the hacked bough
of ash that even dying shivers forth gaily its barrowloads of leaves.

Jack Clemo

Not that I forget, but that, increasingly, the objects of my memory
become ripe for disparagement: irrational or petit bourgeois,
complicit in imperial power, conjurors of air
slapped down by wolfish lecturers with gestures of ennui,
pared nails and implacable smiles, vicious with piety.
Little traitor, I defend them with a wounded stare and no more –
perhaps, I find my place among them, being so cold and all.
Bone-white pits of china clay gouged through
that vision, the extravagant gaze of grace balanced upon us,
its soteriology divorced from nature -- something terrifying
in declaration, his unforgiving line like being hunted.
From the steeply banked clay-tips new dumps of refuse clatter
to extend the protectorate of sand, sparse prickles
of mica like fields in snow – above all, the dogma never thaws.

Let there be a chamber wherein no other light comes

And nothing. The day we climbed slowly out of Antequera
through the cloudbase stippled in dew, the lightly slung blue
bells of nazarenes blazed between karst and darkness,
wild rose and orchid, the unaccountable blood of the peony
aching toward a sound that was both forsakenness and longing –
wolves baying somewhere deep in the park –
and I turned to you and wanted to know what next?
Lost, we turned and turned and turned about among the stacks.
Wings drilling the invisible host from cover to cover
alerted us, the cramped and sullen thorns in anguish loomed.
Until, picking our way down a gully deepening into spate,
the fog whitened, glared alarmingly, then lifted in one sweep
from the sheer drop-off of the cliff – we saw
as if through glass the road receding among grey rocks | the citadel.

On Stockbridge Common

(*clouds*)

And in west and cwep:
Adorno: the lyric as self-protecting unit of isolation divorcing
us from others as from nature, – though what I see and feel,
I hope, is neither illusion nor estrangement, but a recension
whose original, delivering truth this is a fallen variant of.
Once set down, áll things are irrevocable in the great economy:
a falling sparrow, a mite, clouds, the shapes of my children –
even thís no *self-restoring immediacy* or ideological conceit,
but something that bears witness to itself through all time.
In a blur, the swallows buckle in mid-air, merrily at slaughter,
urge themselves upon the Sombornes or suffer the feathery
awns of the sedge at their wingtips: I am beside you, among
and between them, against a sky of cracked tempera the stems
of goldenrod grow invisibly light against. Men are like water.

(*clouds*)

Sources, Notes and Quotations

'Simonsburn': Alessandro Moreschi, Italian castrato soprano (1858–1922). He is the only castrato to have had his singing recorded. A number of these recordings survive, including a version of *Hostias et Preces* by Eugenio Terziani.

'Penitential Psalm': The third italicised marginal is a fragment from *Woefully Arrayed* by William Cornysh.

'*Boscombe*': The italicised marginal is from *Death's Warning* by John Lydgate, in Peter C. Jupp and Clare Gittings eds, *Death In England: An Illustrated History* (Manchester University Press, 1999).

'*Coldsong*': The italicised fragment is from 'The Frost Scene' in John Dryden's libretto to Henry Purcell's *King Arthur, or The British Worthy*.

'*Recessionary*': The italicised fragment is from *The Anglo-Saxon Chronicle* (Manuscript D: Cotton Tiberius B IV).

'*Annulment*': The italicised marginal is from Geoffrey Chaucer, *Troilus and Creseide*.

'*Testament*': The italicised fragments are translated from 'Soneto III' from *Cien sonetos de amor*, Pablo Neruda.

'Very Rich Hours': The italicised fragment is from Christine de Pisan's biography of Charles V.

'The Primacy of Physical Pain': The English Electric Lightning was a supersonic interceptor aircraft that saw service between 1959 and 1988. English Electric was subsumed by BAC under government pressure in 1960, which itself became a part of BAe in 1977 before the the creation of BAE Systems in 1999, a company that was dogged by the Al-Yamamah arms scandal.

'*Lines of Geese*': The italicised marginals are taken from various Anglo-Saxon charms, quoted in Lea Olsan, 'The Inscription of Charms in Anglo-Saxon Manuscripts', *Oral Tradition*, XIV, 2 (1999), 401–19.

'*Easter Sunday, Plaza de la Magdalena, Córdoba*': The Spanish fragment is from the Falangist anthem 'Cara al Sol'. The lyrics were written by José Antonio Primo de

Rivera and set to music by Juan de Tallería. Although many of Primo de Rivera's lyrics and poems were typically nationalistic, he did produce at least one extraordinarily sensitive short lyric, 'Soleá'. For the last line, see Ralph Waldo Emerson's essay, 'Experience', from which it is unconsciously – but with almost complete accuracy – lifted.

'Easter Sunday, Plaza de San Lorenzo, Córdoba': *Offenbarsein* ('revealedness') is a concept particularly associated with the neo-orthodox Protestant theologian Karl Barth's doctrine of the Trinity.

'Easter Sunday, Plaza de San Rafael, Córdoba': The italicised fragment is from *Gretchen am Spinnrade*, a selection of text from Goethe's *Faust* set to music by Schubert as a Lied. The second line of this text, *Mein Herz ist schwer*, mirrors Luther's translation of part of Jeremiah 31:20 – *Darum bricht mir mein Herz* – which was used, in part, as a textual basis for Japanese theologian Kazoh Kitamori's *Theology of the Pain of God*.

'Patricia Beer': English poet and critic (1919–1999) born into a family of Plymouth Brethren. She taught English literature at the Universities of Padua and Rome between 1947 and 1953 before finally settling at Upottery, Devon.

'Fay Pomerance': Anglo-Jewish artist from Birmingham (1912–2001) who completed a number of large cycles, perhaps most notably *The Sphere of Redemption*, parts of which are currently in the collection of the University of Durham. Conroy Maddox (1912–2005): British surrealist painter and atheist who protested against one of Pomerance's exhibitions in Birmingham due to its use of religious iconography. The italicised phrases are taken from *The Scandalous Eye: The Surrealism of Conroy Maddox* by Silvano Levy (Liverpool University Press, 2003). The painting referred to in the second verse is Albrecht Altdorfer's *Crucifixion* (*c.* 1512), of which there are several – the one cited is in the Staatliche Museen, Berlin, and features the donors kneeling at the foot of the cross.

'Jack Clemo': English poet and novelist (1916–1994) who became deaf at twenty and blind at around forty. In the early part of his life a dogmatic Calvinist, he wrote extensively on the doctrines of Election and Irresistible Grace, particularly in the context of a radical antagonism with the natural world – see, for example, his poems 'Christ in the Clay-pit', 'The Clay-Tip Worker' and 'The Broadening Spring', among many others. The italicised marginal is from *Magia Naturalis* by Giambattista della

Porta. In the line 'Lost, we turned and turned and turned about among the stacks,' cf. this fragment from Melanie Challenger's poem, 'Claymore or *Anticipation*':

> Tipping the tongue, the earth passes between them
> As a child brought to the bed of sweet-nothings,
> Seeding in the soft filth of our vernacular. We come
> Against the North Sea's paternity, its long arm of seethings
> And trivial detail – the sea is no mightier, for all its sum,
> Than our turn and turn about among the grazings
> Of Runswick. In the distance, a mechanical plough hums,
> Reprising the tide's eagre – and the soil ended sings
> As we, too, sing through the soil on our tongues.

And this from Challenger's 'Stac Pollaidh or *Regret*':

> Grizzled as a newborn child lying in my arms
> At the uncreated heart of the mountain-top.
> Pretty heart-shaped stack, scar of hours on the land,
> By each footfall ingraining springtimes that weren't mine
> But part of another's stroke and echo —
> Now there's little time left for our delight, and the bleached
> Eggs into which we bite against these pricks of snow
> Unclose their gold and sterile hearths.

'*On Stockbridge Common*': The italicised fragment is from Theodor Adorno's *Lyric Poetry and Society*.

(*clouds*)

,　　　　　　　　,

　　　　　　　　,

,

　　　　,　　　　　　　　　·

　　,　　　　　　　　,

,

　　　　　　　,

　　　　,　　　　　　　　·

,　　　　　,　　　　,

　　　,　　　　　　　　　　,

　　　　　　　　　　　　,

　　　　,　　　　　　　　　　:

　　　　　,

　　　,　　　　　　·

(*clouds*)